PERSONAL FINANCE FOR ADULTS

Financial impact of marriage, parenthood and divorce

William Hoffman

TABLE OF CONTENTS

INTRODUCTION

Life is a journey filled with significant milestones that can have a profound impact on our financial well-being. From the joyous union of marriage to the challenges of parenthood and the complexities of divorce, each of these life events carries its own set of financial implications.

Understanding how these milestones can shape our financial landscape is essential for making informed decisions and planning for the future. In this guide, we will explore the financial impact of marriage, parenthood, and divorce, offering valuable insights and practical tips for managing your finances through these life-changing events.

Whether you're about to embark on a new chapter in your life or are already navigating the challenges of change, this guide will provide you with the knowledge and resources to make sound financial choices and navigate the twists and turns that life may bring.

PURPOSE OF GUIDE

The purpose of this guide is to provide individuals with a comprehensive understanding of the financial impact of major life events, specifically focusing on marriage, parenthood, and divorce. The guide aims to:

1. *Educate: It aims to educate readers about the financial implications and considerations associated with these life events. By providing valuable information and insights, the guide helps individuals make informed decisions and take proactive steps to manage their finances effectively.*

2. ***Empower***: *The guide aims to empower individuals by equipping them with the knowledge and tools necessary to navigate the financial challenges and opportunities that arise from these life events. It provides practical tips, strategies, and considerations to help individuals make sound financial choices and plan for their future.*

3. ***Encourage Planning***: *Planning is crucial when it comes to managing the financial impact of major life events. The guide emphasizes the importance of proactive financial planning and offers guidance on creating budgets, setting financial goals,*

and making informed financial decisions specific to each life event.

4. **Mitigate Challenges**: *Major life events can bring financial challenges and uncertainties. By addressing potential challenges and highlighting strategies to mitigate them, the guide aims to help individuals navigate these events more smoothly and minimize negative financial consequences.*

5. **Promote Financial Well-being**: *Ultimately, the guide seeks to promote financial well-being and stability. It provides insights into how individuals can*

*optimize their financial situation,
protect their assets, plan for the
future, and achieve their long-
term financial goals while
experiencing major life events.*

By fulfilling these purposes, this guide
intends to support individuals in
managing the financial impact of major
life events effectively, enabling them to
make informed decisions and take
control of their financial future.

IMPORTANCE OF UNDERSTANDING FINANCIAL IMPACT

Understanding the financial impact of major life events is of paramount importance for several reasons:

1. *Making Informed Decisions*: Major life events often involve significant financial decisions that can have long-term consequences. By understanding the financial impact, individuals can make informed choices regarding matters such as joint finances, investments, insurance, and estate planning. This knowledge enables them to make decisions aligned with their goals and values.

2. *Financial Planning and Goal Setting*: Awareness of the financial implications allows individuals to incorporate these factors into their overall financial planning. They can assess their current financial situation, set realistic goals, and develop strategies to achieve them. Understanding the financial impact helps individuals create budgets, allocate resources, and prioritize their financial objectives accordingly.

3. *Avoiding Financial Stress and Challenges*: Lack of understanding about the financial impact of major life events can lead to financial stress and

challenges. It may result in unexpected expenses, inadequate savings, or financial strain. By being aware of the potential impacts, individuals can anticipate and plan for these changes, reducing the likelihood of financial difficulties and enhancing their financial resilience.

4. **Maximizing Financial Opportunities**: Major life events can also present financial opportunities. For example, marriage may allow for shared expenses and potential tax benefits, while parenthood may offer access to tax credits and savings programs. Understanding these opportunities enables individuals to leverage them

effectively, optimizing their financial situation and potentially enhancing their wealth.

5. ***Protecting Financial Security****: Major life events can have a profound impact on an individual's financial security. Understanding the financial implications helps individuals protect their assets, manage risks, and make decisions that support long-term financial stability. It allows individuals to consider factors such as insurance coverage, estate planning, and retirement savings, ensuring their financial well-being and that of their loved ones.*

6. ***Adjusting Financial Plans:***
Major life events often require adjustments to existing financial plans. By understanding the financial impact, individuals can reassess their goals, revise their plans, and make necessary changes to accommodate new circumstances. This adaptability helps individuals stay on track towards their financial objectives, even as their life circumstances evolve.

In summary, understanding the financial impact of major life events is crucial for making informed decisions, planning effectively, mitigating financial challenges, maximizing opportunities, protecting financial security, and adapting financial plans to changing circumstances. It empowers individuals to take control of their finances and work towards their desired financial outcomes.

OVERVIEW OF MAJOR LIFE EVENTS

Major life events are significant milestones that individuals commonly experience throughout their lives. These events often have a profound impact on various aspects, including personal, emotional, and financial aspects. Here is an overview of three major life events: marriage, parenthood, and divorce.

1. Marriage:

   - Marriage is the legal and emotional union between two individuals.

   - *Financial implications include*:

- **Combining finances**: Joint bank accounts, shared expenses, and financial decision-making.

- **Tax implications**: Filing taxes jointly or separately, potential tax benefits or liabilities.

- **Estate planning**: Establishing wills, power of attorney, and beneficiary designations.

- **Insurance considerations**: Reviewing and updating health, life, and property insurance.

- **Credit impact**: Jointly managing and building credit profiles.

- **Financial planning**: Setting shared financial goals, budgeting, and investment decisions.

2. Parenthood:

- Parenthood refers to the experience of raising children.

- *Financial implications include*:

- **Budgeting for child-related expenses**: Necessities like food, clothing, and childcare.

- **Childcare and education costs**: Evaluating options, such as daycare, private school, and college savings.

- **Health insurance and medical expenses**: Adding children to insurance coverage, managing healthcare costs.

- **Tax benefits and credits**: Claiming deductions, exemptions, and child tax credits.

- **Estate planning and guardianship**: Appointing guardians and establishing trusts for children.

- **Saving for college education**: Exploring options like 529 plans or other education savings accounts.

- **Balancing parenthood and retirement savings**: Prioritizing retirement savings while addressing immediate child-related expenses.

3. Divorce:

- Divorce is the legal dissolution of a marriage.

- *Financial implications include*:

- **Division of assets and debts**: Evaluating and dividing joint property, investments, and debts.

- **Alimony and child support**: Determining financial support for the spouse and children.

- ***Impact on retirement savings***: Assessing and potentially adjusting retirement plans due to division of assets.

- ***Tax implications of divorce***: Understanding tax consequences related to alimony, property transfers, and filing status changes.

- ***Reviewing and updating financial plans***: Reevaluating financial goals, budgeting, and investment strategies.

- ***Rebuilding credit and financial stability***: Managing individual finances, establishing new credit profiles if needed.

Each major life event has its unique financial considerations and implications. Understanding these impacts helps individuals navigate the

financial aspects associated with each
event, make informed decisions, and
plan for their financial well-being
during and after these transitions.

MARRIAGE AND FINANCIAL IMPACT

Marriage is a significant milestone that not only brings emotional and personal fulfillment but also has a substantial impact on one's financial situation. Combining two lives often means merging finances, assets, and liabilities, which can have both immediate and long-term implications.

One immediate financial effect of marriage is the combined income and expenses of the couple. While dual incomes can provide greater financial stability, it also requires careful budgeting and financial planning to ensure that both partners' goals and priorities are met.

Moreover, marriage can affect taxes, insurance, and estate planning. Couples may be eligible for certain tax benefits and deductions, but they may also face changes in their tax filing status and potential adjustments to their tax liabilities. Additionally, insurance needs may change after marriage, and couples may need to review and update their health insurance, life insurance, and disability coverage.

Estate planning is another critical consideration for married couples, and creating or updating wills, trusts, and other documents can help ensure that each partner's assets are distributed according to their wishes and that their spouse and any children are provided for in the event of death.

On a positive note, marriage can also foster more disciplined financial habits, such as joint financial goal setting, enhanced savings opportunities, and shared responsibilities for managing household finances. Establishing a strong financial foundation early in the marriage can set the stage for a secure and prosperous future together.

Overall, the financial impact of marriage can be both complex and rewarding. It often requires open communication, careful planning, and a willingness to adapt to new financial realities as a couple.

COMBINING FINANCES

Combining finances is a common practice for married couples, and it involves merging or coordinating various aspects of their financial lives. Some key considerations when combining finances:

1. *Open Communication*: Before combining finances, it is crucial for couples to have open and honest communication about their financial situations, goals, and spending habits. Discussing financial expectations, values, and priorities helps establish a solid foundation for managing joint finances.

2. *__Joint or Separate Accounts__*:
   Couples can choose to have a combination of joint and separate bank accounts based on their preferences and circumstances. Joint accounts can be used for shared expenses, such as rent/mortgage payments, utilities, and groceries. Separate accounts can provide individuals with autonomy for personal expenses and discretionary spending.

3. *__Establishing Joint Accounts__*:
   If couples decide to open joint bank accounts, they should visit the bank together and complete the necessary paperwork. Joint accounts allow both individuals

*to have equal access to funds
and simplify the management of
shared expenses.*

4. ***Creating a Budget****: Developing
a joint budget is essential for
managing shared finances
effectively. Couples should
outline their income, expenses,
and savings goals. A budget
helps track spending, identify
areas for potential savings, and
ensure that financial resources
are allocated appropriately.*

5. ***Division of Financial
Responsibilities****: Couples
should discuss and divide
financial responsibilities based on
their individual strengths,*

interests, and availability. This may include tasks such as paying bills, monitoring accounts, and tracking expenses. Clear communication and shared responsibility help maintain financial transparency and accountability.

6. ***Shared Financial Goals****: Couples should identify their shared financial goals, such as saving for a down payment on a home, paying off debt, or planning for retirement. Setting specific, measurable, achievable, relevant, and time-bound (SMART) goals can guide their financial decisions and motivate them to work together towards their objectives.*

7. *Financial Planning and
   Review*: Regularly reviewing
   and adjusting the joint financial
   plan is important as
   circumstances change. Couples
   should revisit their budget,
   savings strategies, and
   investment plans periodically. It
   is also advisable to periodically
   consult with a financial advisor
   who can provide guidance
   tailored to their specific financial
   situation and goals.

8. *Maintaining Individual
   Financial Independence:*
   While combining finances, it is
   also important to respect
   individual financial
   independence. Each partner
   should have some discretionary

*funds that they can use for
personal expenses or savings
without needing to consult the
other person.*

Remember, there is no one-size-fits-all
approach to combining finances in a
marriage. Couples should find a
system that works best for them based
on their unique circumstances, values,
and preferences. Open communication,
mutual respect, and shared financial
goals are the foundation for
successfully managing joint finances.

JOINT BANK ACCOUNT AND BUDGETING

Joint bank accounts and budgeting are important aspects of combining finances in a marriage or any shared financial arrangement. A closer look at joint bank accounts and budgeting:

JOINT BANK ACCOUNTS:

1. *Convenience and Transparency: Joint bank accounts provide a consolidated approach to managing shared finances. They allow both partners to deposit income, pay bills, and track expenses from a single account. It promotes transparency as both individuals*

can easily monitor the account activity.

2. **Shared Expenses**: *Joint accounts are typically used to cover shared expenses, such as rent or mortgage payments, utilities, groceries, and other household bills. By pooling funds into a joint account, couples can ensure that these expenses are covered efficiently and avoid confusion or disputes over who pays for what.*

3. **Communication and Financial Partnership**: *Joint bank accounts foster communication and financial partnership between couples. Regularly*

reviewing account statements and transactions together helps in staying updated on the financial status and facilitates joint decision-making about money matters.

4. ***Financial Responsibility and Trust:*** *By sharing a bank account, couples demonstrate a mutual commitment to financial responsibility and trust. It requires open communication and trust in each other's financial behavior, including responsible spending, avoiding excessive debt, and maintaining financial transparency.*

5. *Individual and Joint Contributions*: Couples can decide on the proportion of their incomes they contribute to the joint account. This can be based on their respective earning capacities or other agreed-upon arrangements. It's important to establish clear expectations and ensure fairness in contributing to shared expenses.

BUDGETING:

1. *Establishing a Joint Budget:* Creating a joint budget is crucial for managing shared finances effectively. It involves identifying income sources, tracking expenses, and setting financial goals together. The budget should encompass both fixed expenses (rent/mortgage,

utilities) and variable expenses (groceries, entertainment).

2. **Allocating Funds**: Budgeting helps allocate funds for various categories, such as housing, transportation, food, debt repayment, savings, and discretionary spending. Couples can agree on how much to allocate to each category based on their priorities and financial goals.

3. *Prioritizing Financial Goals*: Budgeting allows couples to align their financial goals and work towards achieving them together. These goals may include saving for a down

payment on a home, paying off debt, building an emergency fund, or saving for retirement. Prioritizing goals helps in allocating resources accordingly.

4. **Tracking Expenses**: *Regularly tracking expenses is essential to ensure adherence to the budget. Couples can use tools like spreadsheets, budgeting apps, or online banking tools to monitor their spending. This helps identify areas where adjustments may be needed and promotes accountability for financial decisions.*

5. **Regular Budget Reviews**: *Revisit the budget periodically to*

evaluate its effectiveness and make necessary adjustments. Life circumstances and financial goals can change, and the budget should be flexible enough to accommodate these changes. Regular reviews also provide an opportunity for open communication about financial matters.

Remember that joint bank accounts and budgeting require ongoing communication, trust, and shared responsibility. It's important for couples to regularly discuss their financial situation, make joint decisions, and support each other in achieving their financial goals.

TAX IMPLICATIONS

Tax implications are an important consideration when it comes to various life events and financial decisions. Some key tax implications to be aware of:

1. *Filing Status*: Your marital status determines your filing status for tax purposes. If you are married, you can choose to file jointly or separately. Filing jointly often offers more favorable tax rates and deductions, but it's important to compare the tax benefits of both options to determine the most advantageous choice for your specific situation.

2. ***Income Tax***: *When you're married, your combined income may push you into a higher tax bracket. This is known as the "marriage penalty." Conversely, in some cases, being married can result in a tax advantage due to income splitting and lower tax rates for joint filers. It's essential to assess the impact of your combined income on your tax liability and explore tax planning strategies accordingly.*

3. ***Deductions and Credits***: *Marriage can affect the deductions and credits available to you. Some common deductions and credits impacted by marital status include the standard deduction, child tax*

credits, education-related credits, and certain itemized deductions. Married couples should review and understand the tax implications of these deductions and credits to maximize their tax savings.

4. **Health Insurance**: *Marriage may provide an opportunity to reassess your health insurance coverage. You may explore whether it is more advantageous to be covered under a joint health insurance plan or maintain individual plans. Consider factors such as coverage, premiums, and subsidies to make an informed decision.*

5. ***Estate and Gift Taxes:***
   Marriage can have implications for estate and gift taxes. Transfers of assets between spouses are generally tax-free, allowing for estate planning strategies that can minimize the potential tax liability upon the death of one spouse. Understanding the estate and gift tax rules and considering appropriate planning measures can help you preserve wealth for future generations.

6. ***Retirement Contributions:***
   Being married can affect retirement contributions and tax planning. If one spouse is not employed or has limited income, they may still be eligible to contribute to an individual

retirement account (IRA) based on their spouse's income. This is known as a spousal IRA contribution. Additionally, married couples may have different retirement account options and contribution limits, which should be considered when planning for retirement savings.

7. ***State and Local Taxes:*** *It's important to consider the state and local tax implications of marriage. Each state has its own tax laws and regulations, which may have different rules for married couples. Reviewing state and local tax laws can help you understand how your marital status impacts your tax liability at the state and local levels.*

It's important to consult with a tax professional or utilize tax software to fully understand the tax implications specific to your situation. They can provide personalized guidance and help you navigate the complexities of the tax code to optimize your tax planning and compliance.

ESTATE PLANNING AND BENEFICIARY DESIGNATION

Estate planning and beneficiary designation are crucial aspects of financial planning, especially in the context of marriage. Here's an overview of these concepts:

ESTATE PLANNING:

1. ***Wills****: A will is a legal document that outlines your wishes for the distribution of your assets after your death. In a will, you can specify how your property, investments, and personal belongings should be distributed among your beneficiaries. It is important for married couples to*

have updated wills that reflect their current wishes.

2. ***Trusts****: Trusts are legal arrangements that allow you to transfer assets to a trustee to manage and distribute them according to your instructions. Trusts can provide various benefits, such as avoiding probate, minimizing estate taxes, and providing for the management of assets for minor children or beneficiaries with special needs.*

3. ***Power of Attorney****: A power of attorney is a legal document that designates someone to make financial or healthcare decisions*

on your behalf if you become incapacitated. It is recommended to have powers of attorney in place to ensure that your spouse or a trusted individual can act on your behalf in case of incapacity.

4. ***Healthcare Directives****: Healthcare directives, such as a living will or healthcare power of attorney, outline your wishes regarding medical treatment and end-of-life care. These documents ensure that your healthcare decisions are respected and that your spouse or designated individual can make healthcare choices on your behalf if you are unable to do so.*

BENEFICIARY DESIGNATIONS:

1. *Retirement Accounts:* Retirement accounts, such as IRAs, 401(k)s, and pensions, allow you to designate beneficiaries who will inherit those assets upon your death. Review and update beneficiary designations regularly to ensure they align with your current wishes, especially after significant life events like marriage.

2. *Life Insurance Policies*: Life insurance policies also require beneficiary designations. You can designate your spouse as the primary beneficiary, ensuring that they receive the death benefit if you pass away. Additionally, you can name contingent or secondary

beneficiaries to receive the benefit if your spouse predeceases you.

3. ***Bank and Investment Accounts****: Many bank and investment accounts allow you to designate beneficiaries who will inherit the assets held in those accounts upon your death. Review and update beneficiary designations on these accounts to ensure they reflect your current intentions.*

It is important to regularly review and update your estate planning documents and beneficiary designations to ensure they align with your current wishes, particularly after

significant life events such as
marriage, divorce, or the birth of a
child. Consult with an estate planning
attorney or a financial advisor who
specializes in estate planning to ensure
your documents are legally sound and
meet your specific needs.

INSURANCE CONSIDERATIONS

Insurance considerations are an important part of financial planning, and they help protect you, your loved ones, and your assets from unexpected events. Some key insurance considerations to keep in mind:

1. *Life Insurance*: Life insurance provides a death benefit to your beneficiaries upon your passing. If you are married, having life insurance can help ensure that your spouse is financially protected in the event of your death. The coverage amount should be sufficient to cover ongoing expenses, outstanding debts, and future financial needs. It's important to assess your

specific circumstances and consult with a financial advisor or insurance professional to determine the appropriate coverage amount and type of policy (such as term or permanent life insurance).

2. **Health Insurance**: *Health insurance is essential to cover medical expenses and protect against the financial burden of healthcare costs. If you're married, you may have the option to be covered under one spouse's employer-sponsored health insurance plan or seek coverage through a private plan. Compare the coverage, premiums, deductibles, and out-of-pocket costs to select the*

most suitable health insurance option for you and your spouse.

3. ***Disability Insurance***: *Disability insurance provides income replacement if you become unable to work due to a disability. It's important to have disability insurance coverage to protect your income and financial stability. Assess your needs and consider both short-term and long-term disability insurance policies. Some employers offer disability insurance as part of their benefits package, but you may also need to explore individual policies to supplement your coverage.*

4. ***Homeowners/Renters Insurance***: *Homeowners insurance protects your home and its contents against damage or loss due to perils such as fire, theft, or natural disasters. If you're married and own a home together, review your homeowners insurance policy to ensure it adequately covers your property and belongings. If you're renting, consider renters insurance to protect your personal belongings and provide liability coverage.*

5. ***Auto Insurance***: *Auto insurance is necessary to protect against financial loss in case of accidents, theft, or damage to your vehicles. If you and your spouse own vehicles, combine your auto insurance policies or explore multi-car discounts to potentially reduce premiums.*

Review the coverage limits, deductibles, and types of coverage (such as liability, collision, and comprehensive) to ensure they align with your needs.

6. ***Umbrella Insurance****: Umbrella insurance provides additional liability coverage beyond the limits of your other insurance policies, such as homeowners and auto insurance. It offers broader protection and higher coverage limits, which can be beneficial for married couples with higher net worth or increased liability exposure. Consult with an insurance professional to assess whether umbrella insurance is appropriate for your circumstances.*

Remember to regularly review your insurance policies, coverage amounts, and beneficiaries to ensure they align with your changing circumstances. Life events such as marriage, the birth of a child, or the purchase of a new home may necessitate adjustments to your insurance coverage. Consult with an Insurance professional or financial advisor to assess your specific insurance needs and determine the most suitable coverage options for you and your spouse.

IMPACT ON CREDIT SCORES

Various factors can impact credit scores, and some of those factors can be influenced by marriage or shared financial arrangements. Here's a look at how marriage can affect credit scores:

1. *Joint Accounts: Opening joint accounts, such as joint credit cards or loans, can impact credit scores. Payment history and credit utilization on these joint accounts will be reflected on both spouses' credit reports. If payments are made on time and credit utilization is kept low, it can positively impact credit scores. Conversely, missed payments or high credit*

utilization can have a negative effect.

2. **Credit History**: When you get married, your credit history remains separate. However, joint financial activities, such as applying for a mortgage or car loan together, will be reflected on both spouses' credit reports. If one spouse has a strong credit history and the other has a limited or poor credit history, it may affect the couple's ability to secure favorable loan terms.

3. **Authorized User Accounts**: Adding a spouse as an authorized user on an existing credit card can potentially benefit

their credit score if the primary cardholder has a positive payment history and low credit utilization. However, if the primary cardholder's credit behavior is negative, such as late payments or high balances, it could negatively impact the authorized user's credit score as well.

4. **Co-Signing Loans**: *Co-signing a loan with your spouse means that you are equally responsible for the debt. The loan will appear on both credit reports, and any missed payments or defaults can harm both credit scores. On the other hand, consistent on-time payments can benefit both credit scores.*

5. *Name Changes:* If you or your
   spouse change your last name
   after marriage, it's important to
   update your personal information
   with creditors and credit
   bureaus. This ensures that your
   credit history is accurately
   reported and linked to your new
   name.

6. *Individual Credit Behavior:*
   While marriage can involve
   shared financial responsibilities,
   each spouse's individual credit
   behavior continues to have an
   impact on their credit scores.
   Paying bills on time, keeping
   credit card balances low, and
   maintaining a diverse credit mix
   are positive credit habits that
   should be maintained
   individually.

It's essential to regularly monitor your credit reports from the major credit bureaus (Equifax, Experian, and TransUnion) to ensure accuracy and address any discrepancies. Additionally, open communication with your spouse about financial goals, responsible credit behavior, and joint financial decisions can help maintain and improve credit scores over time.

Remember that credit scores are just one aspect of your overall financial health. Responsible financial management, including budgeting, saving, and avoiding excessive debt, is crucial for long-term financial well-being, regardless of the impact on credit scores.

FINANCIAL PLANNING FOR FUTURE GOALS

Financial planning is crucial for achieving future goals and ensuring long-term financial stability. Some steps to consider when creating a financial plan for future goals:

1. ***Set Clear and Specific Goals:*** *Identify your future financial goals, such as buying a home, saving for retirement, funding education, starting a business, or traveling. Make sure your goals are specific, measurable, achievable, relevant, and time-bound (SMART goals).*

2. ***Assess Your Current Financial Situation***: *Evaluate your current financial situation by examining your income, expenses, assets, liabilities, and cash flow. Understand your net worth and determine how much you can allocate toward your future goals.*

3. ***Create a Budget***: *Establish a budget to allocate your income toward your goals, savings, and expenses. Track your spending, prioritize essential expenses, and identify areas where you can cut back to save more for your future goals.*

4. *__Emergency Fund__: Build an emergency fund to cover unexpected expenses or income disruptions. Aim to save three to six months' worth of living expenses in a liquid and easily accessible account.*

5. *__Debt Management__: Develop a plan to manage and pay off any existing debts, such as credit card debt, student loans, or car loans. Prioritize high-interest debts while making minimum payments on others. Consider debt consolidation or refinancing options to lower interest rates and simplify repayment.*

6. *Saving and Investing:*
   Determine the amount you need
   to save regularly to achieve your
   future goals. Consider the time
   horizon, risk tolerance, and
   investment options suitable for
   each goal. Explore savings
   accounts, certificates of deposit
   (CDs), individual retirement
   accounts (IRAs), employer-
   sponsored retirement plans (e.g.,
   401(k)), and other investment
   vehicles.

7. *Insurance Coverage:* Review
   your insurance coverage to
   protect yourself and your family
   from potential risks. This
   includes health insurance, life
   insurance, disability insurance,
   homeowners/renters insurance,

and auto insurance. Ensure that the coverage aligns with your needs and provides adequate protection.

8. **Retirement Planning**: Plan for retirement by estimating your future financial needs, considering factors such as desired lifestyle, healthcare costs, and inflation. Maximize contributions to retirement accounts, take advantage of employer matches, and explore investment options that align with your retirement goals.

9. **Tax Planning**: Understand the tax implications of your financial decisions and explore strategies

that can minimize your tax liability. This includes maximizing deductions, utilizing tax-advantaged accounts, and consulting with a tax professional to optimize your tax planning.

10.   **Regular Review and Adjustments**: *Regularly review and reassess your financial plan. Life circumstances, goals, and economic conditions can change, requiring adjustments to your plan. Stay informed about financial trends, seek professional advice when needed, and make necessary modifications to keep your plan on track.*

Remember, financial planning is a dynamic process that requires ongoing monitoring and adjustments. It is valuable to seek guidance from financial advisors or professionals who can provide personalized advice based on your specific situation, goals, and risk tolerance.

PARENTHOOD AND FINANCIAL IMPACT

Parenthood is a profound and transformative journey that brings immeasurable joy and fulfillment, but it also introduces significant financial responsibilities and challenges. From pregnancy and childbirth to raising children through various life stages, the financial impact of parenthood can be substantial.

The costs associated with pregnancy, childbirth, and early childhood development can place a strain on a family's finances. Medical expenses, childcare costs, and a potential reduction in income due to maternity or paternity leave are just a few of the financial considerations that new parents must navigate.

As children grow, the financial implications expand to include education, extracurricular activities, healthcare, and everyday expenses. Planning for these costs requires foresight and careful budgeting to ensure that parents can provide for their children's needs while still securing their own financial future.

Saving for college education is a particularly important consideration for many parents. The rising costs of higher education make it essential for parents to start saving early and explore various savings vehicles, such as 529 college savings plans, to help mitigate the financial burden of tuition and related expenses.

Furthermore, parents often need to reassess their insurance coverage, estate planning, and overall financial strategy to account for their children's well-being and future needs. Life insurance, disability insurance, and guardianship designations are key components of a comprehensive financial plan for parents.

Despite the financial challenges, parenthood can also bring a renewed focus on financial stability, long-term planning, and legacy building. Many parents find inspiration in providing a secure and prosperous future for their children, motivating them to make

prudent financial decisions and
investments.

In summary, the financial impact of
parenthood requires careful planning,
budgeting, and a steadfast
commitment to providing for the needs
and aspirations of the entire family.
While it may present challenges,
parenthood also offers opportunities
for personal and financial growth.

BUDGETING FOR CHILD RELATED EXPENSES

Budgeting for child-related expenses is crucial for managing your finances effectively. Some steps to consider when creating a budget for child-related expenses:

1. *Identify and Prioritize Expenses: Make a list of all the child-related expenses you anticipate, such as childcare, education, healthcare, clothing, food, extracurricular activities, and more. Prioritize these expenses based on their importance and estimated costs.*

2. ***Review Your Current Budget***: *Evaluate your existing budget and identify areas where you can allocate funds for child-related expenses. Look for potential savings by cutting back on discretionary spending or reallocating funds from non-essential categories.*

3. ***Estimate Costs***: *Research and estimate the costs of various child-related expenses. Consider factors such as age, location, lifestyle, and personal preferences. Look for average costs in your area and seek input from other parents or online resources to get a realistic estimate.*

4. *Create a Child-Related Expense Category*: Establish a separate budget category specifically for child-related expenses. This will help you track and manage these expenses more effectively. Allocate a portion of your monthly income to this category.

5. *Childcare Costs*: Childcare expenses can be significant. Research the cost of daycare centers, nannies, or babysitters in your area. Determine which option aligns with your needs and budget. Consider whether you qualify for any government assistance programs or employer-provided benefits related to childcare.

6. ***Education Expenses***: *Plan for education expenses, including school fees, uniforms, books, and supplies. If you anticipate private school or college costs, start saving early by setting up a dedicated education savings account, such as a 529 college savings plan.*

7. ***Healthcare Costs***: *Account for healthcare expenses, including regular check-ups, vaccinations, and potential medical treatments. Review your health insurance coverage to understand the out-of-pocket costs associated with your child's healthcare needs.*

8. *Clothing and Supplies:*
Estimate the costs of clothing,
shoes, diapers, and other
essential supplies for your child.
Take into account growth spurts
and seasonal needs when
budgeting for clothing expenses.

9. *Extracurricular Activities:*
Consider the costs of
extracurricular activities such as
sports, music lessons, art
classes, or other hobbies your
child may pursue. Research the
fees and equipment costs
associated with these activities
and include them in your budget.

10. ***Adjust and Review Regularly****: Regularly review and adjust your child-related expense budget as your child grows and their needs change. Reassess and reallocate funds as necessary to ensure your budget remains realistic and aligned with your financial goals.*

Remember, every family's financial situation is unique, and your budget should reflect your specific circumstances. It's important to regularly track your expenses, monitor your budget, and make adjustments as needed. Adapting to changes and being flexible with your budgeting approach will help you manage child-related expenses effectively.

CHILDCARE AND EDUCATION COST

Childcare and education costs are significant expenses for parents. Here's a breakdown of these expenses and some strategies to manage them:

CHILDCARE COSTS:

1. **Research Options**: Explore different childcare options such as daycare centers, home-based daycares, nannies, or babysitters. Compare costs and quality of care to find the best fit for your child and budget.

2. **Government Assistance**: Check if you qualify for government assistance programs such as child care subsidies or tax credits to help offset the costs.

3. **Flexible Spending Accounts (FSAs)**: If available through your employer, utilize FSAs to set aside pre-tax dollars for eligible childcare expenses, reducing your taxable income.

4. **Shared Care**: Consider sharing childcare responsibilities with family members or trusted friends. This arrangement can help reduce costs and provide social interaction for your child.

5. **Negotiate Fees**: When discussing childcare arrangements, negotiate fees with providers. They may be open to adjusting rates based on your specific needs.

6. **Tax Benefits**: Take advantage of tax benefits related to childcare, such as the Child and Dependent Care Tax Credit, which can help reduce your tax liability.

EDUCATION COSTS:

1. **Start Saving Early**: Begin saving for your child's education as soon as possible. Consider options like 529 college savings plans, which offer tax advantages and investment growth potential.

2. **Research School Options**: Evaluate different educational institutions, including public, private, and charter schools. Compare tuition fees and associated expenses to find the best educational fit within your budget.

3. **Scholarships and Grants**: Research scholarships, grants, and financial aid options available to students. Start exploring these opportunities as early as possible to

maximize your chances of receiving assistance.

4. **Education Savings Accounts**: Investigate education savings accounts, such as Coverdell Education Savings Accounts (ESAs), which allow tax-advantaged savings for qualified education expenses.

5. **Consider Community College or Trade Schools**: Community colleges or trade schools often offer more affordable educational options compared to four-year universities. Explore these alternatives based on your child's career goals.

6. **Encourage Financial Responsibility**: Teach your child about the value of education and the importance of balancing costs. Encourage them to pursue scholarships, part-time jobs, or

internships to help cover educational
expenses.

Remember to regularly review your
budget, adjust your savings goals, and
explore opportunities to optimize your
childcare and education expenses.
Financial planning and early
preparation can help alleviate the
financial burden and provide your child
with quality care and education.

HEALTH INSURANCE AND MEDICAL EXPENSES

Health insurance and medical expenses are critical considerations in financial planning. Some key points to keep in mind:

HEALTH INSURANCE:

1. **Evaluate Coverage Options**: Research and compare health insurance plans to find the one that meets your family's needs. Consider factors such as premiums, deductibles, copayments, out-of-pocket maximums, network coverage, and the range of benefits provided.

2. **Employer-Sponsored Plans**: If available, assess the health insurance options provided by your or your

partner's employer. Compare the costs and coverage to determine the most suitable plan for your family.

3. **Government Programs**: Check if you qualify for government programs like Medicaid or the Children's Health Insurance Program (CHIP), which provide healthcare coverage for low-income families and children.

4. **Family Coverage**: Evaluate whether it's more cost-effective to have separate plans for each family member or opt for family coverage that covers all eligible family members under one plan.

5. **Health Savings Accounts (HSAs) and Flexible Spending Accounts (FSAs)**: If offered, take advantage of these tax-advantaged accounts to save for medical expenses. Contributions to HSAs are tax-deductible, and

withdrawals for qualified medical expenses are tax-free.

MEDICAL EXPENSES:

1. **Budget for Routine Expenses:** Account for routine medical expenses such as doctor visits, vaccinations, preventive care, and prescription medications in your budget.

2. **Emergency Fund**: Build an emergency fund to cover unexpected medical expenses or medical emergencies. Aim to save at least three to six months' worth of living expenses.

3. **Understand Your Coverage**: Familiarize yourself with the details of your health insurance plan, including copayments, deductibles, and out-of-pocket maximums. This will help you

understand your financial responsibility for medical services.

4. **Network Providers**: Utilize in-network healthcare providers to maximize your insurance coverage and minimize out-of-pocket expenses. Be aware of any restrictions or requirements regarding referrals or pre-authorization for certain services.

5. **Generic Medications**: Whenever possible, opt for generic medications, as they are usually more affordable than brand-name equivalents. Ask your healthcare provider or pharmacist about generic alternatives.

6. **Negotiate Medical Bills**: If you receive a large medical bill, it's worth contacting the provider to discuss payment options or negotiate the bill. They may be willing to work out a payment plan or offer a discount.

7. **Health Maintenance**: Prioritize preventive care and healthy lifestyle choices to reduce the risk of costly medical conditions in the future.

It's essential to review your health insurance coverage regularly, understand your benefits, and stay informed about changes to your plan. Additionally, keep track of your medical expenses, save receipts, and consult with a tax professional to determine if you qualify for any medical expense deductions or tax credits.

TAX BENEFITS AND CREDITS

Parenthood can bring several tax benefits and credits that can help reduce the financial impact. Some key tax benefits and credits to consider:

1. *Child Tax Credit: The Child Tax Credit is a tax credit that can reduce your tax liability for each qualifying child under the age of 17. The credit amount is up to $2,000 per child, and it may be partially refundable, depending on your income. The American Rescue Plan Act of 2021 temporarily expanded the credit for the tax year 2021, increasing the maximum credit amount and making it fully refundable for many families.*

2. ***Child and Dependent Care
   Credit***: *If you incur expenses for
   childcare or dependent care to
   allow you and your spouse to
   work or look for work, you may
   be eligible for the Child and
   Dependent Care Credit. The
   credit can be up to $3,000 for
   one child or up to $6,000 for two
   or more children. The actual
   credit amount is based on your
   qualifying expenses and your
   income.*

3. ***Earned Income Tax Credit
   (EITC)***: *The EITC is a refundable
   tax credit designed to assist low-
   to-moderate-income working
   individuals and families. The
   credit amount depends on your*

income, filing status, and the number of qualifying children you have. Having a child or multiple children can increase the credit amount you may be eligible for.

4. ***Adoption Tax Credit****: If you've adopted a child, you may be eligible for the Adoption Tax Credit. This credit helps offset qualified adoption expenses, such as adoption fees, court costs, and travel expenses. The credit is subject to income limitations but can be substantial.*

5. ***Education Tax Credits****: As your child progresses in education, you may be eligible for education-related tax credits. The most common ones are the*

American Opportunity Credit and the Lifetime Learning Credit. These credits can help offset qualified education expenses, such as tuition, fees, and required course materials.

6. ***Health Insurance Premium Tax Credit:*** *If you purchase health insurance through the Health Insurance Marketplace and meet certain income requirements, you may be eligible for a premium tax credit. This credit helps reduce the cost of health insurance premiums for you and your family.*

It's crucial to research and understand the specific eligibility requirements, limitations, and any changes to tax laws related to these credits and benefits. Consult with a tax professional or utilize tax software to ensure you take full advantage of the available tax benefits and credits related to parenthood.

ESTATE PLANNING AND GUARDIANSHIP

Parenthood has significant implications for estate planning and guardianship. Some key considerations:

1. ***Will and Testament****: Create a will to outline your wishes regarding the distribution of your assets and the designation of a guardian for your child in the event of your death. A will allows you to have control over who will care for your child and manage their inheritance.*

2. ***Guardianship Designation****: Select a guardian who will assume responsibility for your child's care if both parents pass*

away. Consider factors such as the guardian's willingness, ability to provide a loving and stable environment, and compatibility with your parenting values. Discuss your decision with the potential guardian to ensure their willingness to take on this role.

3. ***Trusts****: Consider setting up a trust to manage and protect your child's inheritance. A trust can provide guidelines on how the funds are used and distributed, ensuring they are used for your child's benefit. You can also designate a trustee to manage the trust on your child's behalf until they reach a specified age or milestone.*

4. *Life Insurance*: Evaluate your
   life insurance coverage to ensure
   it is sufficient to provide financial
   support for your child's needs in
   the event of your death. The
   payout from a life insurance
   policy can help cover ongoing
   expenses, such as childcare,
   education, and healthcare.

5. *Beneficiary Designations*:
   Review and update beneficiary
   designations on retirement
   accounts, investment accounts,
   and life insurance policies to
   ensure they align with your
   wishes. Consider naming a trust
   as the beneficiary if you have
   one in place for your child's
   benefit.

6. ***Advance Healthcare Directive:*** *Create an advance healthcare directive or a medical power of attorney that designates someone to make medical decisions on your behalf if you are unable to do so. Ensure your designated person is aware of your wishes regarding your child's healthcare decisions.*

7. ***Review and Update Regularly:*** *Review your estate plan periodically, especially when major life events occur, such as the birth of another child, divorce, or changes in financial circumstances. Update your plan as necessary to reflect your current wishes and the best interests of your child.*

8. *__Consult an Estate Planning__
   __Attorney__: Seek guidance from
   an estate planning attorney who
   can assess your specific situation
   and help you create a
   comprehensive plan that
   addresses your goals and
   protects your child's well-being.
   They can provide expert advice
   on legal and financial matters
   related to estate planning and
   guardianship.*

Remember, estate planning is a complex and personal process. It's important to consult with professionals and ensure your wishes are legally documented to provide for your child's future and protect their best interests.

SAVING FOR COLLEGE EDUCATION

Parenthood comes with the responsibility of planning for your child's education, including saving for college. Some key considerations for saving for college education:

1. *Start Early:* The sooner you start saving for college, the more time you have to benefit from compound interest and investment growth. Begin saving as early as possible to maximize your savings potential.

2. *Determine Savings Goals:* Estimate the future costs of college education based on

potential tuition rates, inflation, and the number of years until your child starts college. This will help you set realistic savings goals.

3. ***529 College Savings Plans****: Consider opening a 529 college savings plan, which is a tax-advantaged investment account specifically designed for education expenses. Contributions to a 529 plan grow tax-free, and withdrawals used for qualified education expenses are also tax-free. Research and compare different state-sponsored 529 plans to find the one that best suits your needs.*

4. ***Education Savings Accounts (ESAs)****: Another option is an Education Savings Account, also*

known as a Coverdell ESA. Contributions to an ESA grow tax-free, and withdrawals for qualified education expenses are tax-free as well. However, ESA contributions have an annual limit, and there are income restrictions for eligibility. Consult with a financial advisor to determine if an ESA is a suitable option for your situation.

5. ***Automatic Contributions***: *Set up automatic contributions to your college savings account. Regularly contributing even small amounts can accumulate over time and help you reach your savings goals.*

6. ***Explore Investment Options***: Determine your risk tolerance and consider investing your college savings in a diversified portfolio. Consult with a financial advisor to select appropriate investments based on your timeframe and risk profile.

7. ***Scholarships and Grants***: Encourage your child to pursue academic excellence and extracurricular activities that may increase their eligibility for scholarships and grants. Research and apply for scholarships and grants that can help offset college costs.

8. **Consider Other Funding Sources:** Explore other potential funding sources, such as employer-sponsored education assistance programs, work-study opportunities, or part-time jobs your child can pursue during their college years.

9. **Communication and Planning:** Discuss your college savings plan with your child as they get older. Help them understand the importance of saving for their education and involve them in the process. This can encourage a sense of responsibility and ownership over their educational goals.

10. ***Regularly Review and Adjust***: *Periodically review your college savings plan to ensure it aligns with your goals and adjust contributions or investment strategies as needed. Keep track of your progress and make any necessary adjustments along the way.*

Remember, saving for college is a long-term commitment. It's important to establish a realistic savings plan, take advantage of tax-advantaged accounts, and regularly monitor and adjust your savings strategy to ensure you're on track to meet your goals.

BALANCING PARENTHOOD AND RETIREMENT SAVINGS

Parenthood can have a significant impact on retirement savings, as it introduces new financial responsibilities. Balancing parenthood and retirement savings requires careful planning and consideration. Some key points to help you manage both:

1. *Prioritize Retirement Savings: While it's natural to prioritize your child's needs, it's crucial not to neglect your retirement savings. Remember that there are no loans or scholarships available for retirement, so it's essential to save consistently for your future financial security.*

2. ***Create a Budget****: Establish a comprehensive budget that considers both your child-related expenses and retirement savings. This will help you allocate your income effectively and identify areas where you can potentially cut costs or save more.*

3. ***Take Advantage of Employer-Sponsored Retirement Plans****: If your employer offers a retirement plan, such as a 401(k) or a 403(b), contribute at least enough to take full advantage of any matching contributions. Employer matches are essentially free money that*

can significantly boost your retirement savings.

4. ***Automate Retirement Contributions****: Set up automatic contributions to your retirement accounts. This ensures that a portion of your income goes directly into savings, making it easier to consistently save for retirement while managing other expenses.*

5. ***Balance Short-Term and Long-Term Goals****: It's important to strike a balance between your short-term financial obligations as a parent and your long-term retirement goals. Evaluate your financial*

*situation and set realistic savings
targets that allow you to save for
retirement while meeting your
child's immediate needs.*

6. ***Review and Adjust Regularly****:
Periodically review your
retirement savings strategy and
make adjustments as necessary.
As your child grows and financial
circumstances change, reassess
your savings goals and adjust
your contributions accordingly.*

7. ***Educate Your Child about
Financial Responsibility****:
Teach your child about financial
responsibility and the importance
of saving from an early age.
Encourage them to develop good*

*money habits and understand
the value of long-term savings.*

8. ***Seek Professional Advice***: *Consider consulting with a financial advisor who can help you create a comprehensive financial plan that balances your parenthood responsibilities and retirement savings goals. They can provide personalized advice based on your specific circumstances.*

Remember that finding the right balance between parenthood and retirement savings is an ongoing process. It requires regular evaluation, adjustments, and making informed financial decisions. By prioritizing retirement savings, budgeting effectively, and seeking professional advice when needed, you can work towards both providing for your child and securing your future retirement.

DIVORCE AND FINANCIAL IMPACT

Divorce is a significant life event that can have a profound impact on your financial situation. The process of untangling shared assets and liabilities, establishing separate households, and potentially navigating child support and alimony arrangements can create financial complexities that require careful consideration and planning.

One of the immediate financial effects of divorce is the division of assets and debts. This can involve the equitable distribution of property, including real estate, investments, retirement accounts, and personal belongings. Understanding the legal and financial implications of asset division is crucial to securing your financial future post-divorce.

In addition to division of assets, divorce can also impact earning potential and income. Transitioning from a dual-income household to a single-income situation can require adjustments to lifestyle, budgeting, and financial priorities. It's important to evaluate your current financial position and consider how it may change post-divorce.

Child support and alimony can also be significant financial considerations in divorce. Depending on the circumstances, one spouse may be required to provide financial support to the other or to children. Understanding the legal requirements and financial implications of these arrangements is essential for both parties involved.

Furthermore, divorce can have tax implications. Changes in filing status, eligible deductions, and the treatment of assets can all affect your tax situation. Seeking professional tax advice during and after divorce can help you navigate these complexities and optimize your financial position.

Insurance needs may also change after divorce. Reviewing and updating health insurance, life insurance, and other coverage is essential to ensure that you and any dependents are adequately protected. Additionally, estate planning, including wills, trusts, and beneficiary designations, may need to be revised to reflect post-divorce circumstances.

It's important to approach divorce with a clear understanding of your financial standing and a plan for securing your financial future. Seeking the guidance of financial advisors, attorneys, and other professionals can provide invaluable support during this challenging time and help you make informed decisions about your financial well-being post-divorce.

While divorce can bring financial challenges, it also presents an opportunity to reassess your financial goals, values, and priorities. Taking proactive steps to rebuild your financial stability, pursue new opportunities, and shape your financial future in alignment with your individual goals is an important part of the post-divorce journey.

In summary, divorce can have a significant impact on your financial situation, requiring careful consideration and planning to navigate the complexities of asset division, income changes, support arrangements, tax implications, insurance needs, and estate planning. While it may present challenges, divorce also offers an opportunity to reclaim your financial independence and chart a new course for your financial well-being.

OVERVIEW OF THE DIVORCE PROCESS

The divorce process can vary depending on the jurisdiction and the specific circumstances of the couple involved. However, here's a general overview of the divorce process:

1. *Filing the Petition*: The divorce process typically begins with one spouse filing a divorce petition or complaint in the appropriate court. The petition outlines the grounds for divorce (such as irreconcilable differences or fault-based grounds) and may include requests for child custody, spousal support, and division of assets.

2. ***Serving the Petition***: After
filing, the petition must be
served to the other spouse,
usually by a process server or
through certified mail. This
ensures that the other party is
aware of the divorce
proceedings.

3. ***Response and Counterclaim***:
The served spouse has a certain
period, usually 30 days, to
respond to the petition. They
may choose to contest the
divorce, dispute the terms, or file
a counterclaim with their own
requests and allegations.

4. ***Temporary Orders***: During the
divorce process, either spouse

can request temporary orders for issues like child custody, child support, spousal support, and restraining orders. These orders provide guidelines and protections until the final divorce settlement is reached.

5. ***Discovery****: Both parties exchange relevant financial and other information through a process called discovery. This can include financial documents, property valuations, and other evidence that may impact the division of assets, spousal support, and child custody decisions.*

6. ***Negotiation and Mediation****: Many divorcing couples attempt to reach a settlement agreement through negotiation or*

mediation. This involves both parties and their attorneys working together to resolve issues like asset division, support, and custody arrangements outside of court.

7. ***Court Proceedings****: If a settlement cannot be reached through negotiation or mediation, the divorce case may proceed to court. Each spouse presents their case, including evidence and arguments, and the judge makes decisions on contested issues.*

8. ***Finalizing the Divorce****: Once all issues are resolved, either through settlement or court*

proceedings, the divorce can be finalized. The final divorce decree, which outlines the terms of the divorce and any court orders, is issued by the court.

9. ***Post-Divorce Matters****: After the divorce is finalized, there may be ongoing matters to address, such as enforcing court orders, modifying child custody or support arrangements, or resolving any disputes that arise.*

It's important to note that the divorce process can be complex and emotionally challenging. It's advisable for individuals going through a divorce to seek guidance from an attorney who specializes in family law. An

experienced attorney can provide
personalized advice, help navigate the
legal process, and protect your rights
and interests throughout the divorce
proceedings.

DIVISION OF ASSETS AND DEBTS

During a divorce, the division of assets and debts is an important aspect to consider. The specific rules and laws governing asset and debt division can vary depending on the jurisdiction, so it's essential to consult with an attorney familiar with family law in your area. However, here are some general principles:

1. ***Marital Property vs. Separate Property***: *In most jurisdictions, assets and debts acquired during the marriage are considered marital property and are subject to division. Separate property, which typically includes assets acquired before the marriage or*

through inheritance or gifts, may be excluded from division.

2. ***Equitable Distribution****: Many jurisdictions follow the principle of equitable distribution, which means that marital assets and debts are divided in a manner deemed fair and equitable, but not necessarily equal. The court considers various factors, such as the length of the marriage, each spouse's financial contributions, and the needs of each party, when making division decisions.*

3. ***Asset Valuation****: Assets need to be valued before division to determine their worth. This may*

involve appraisals for real estate, businesses, or other valuable assets. Accurate valuation is crucial to ensure a fair distribution.

4. ***Debts and Liabilities****: Marital debts, including mortgages, credit card debts, loans, and other financial obligations, are also subject to division. Debts acquired during the marriage are typically divided in a manner similar to assets, taking into account factors like financial ability and responsibility for incurring the debt.*

5. ***Negotiated Settlement****: In many cases, divorcing couples*

can negotiate a settlement
agreement outside of court.
Through negotiation, they can
agree on how to divide assets
and debts in a way that both
parties find acceptable. This
allows for more control and
flexibility in the division process.

6. *Court Determination:* If the
couple cannot reach a settlement
agreement, the court may step
in to make decisions regarding
asset and debt division. The
court considers relevant factors,
such as the financial
circumstances of each spouse
and the best interests of any
children involved, to determine
an equitable distribution.

7. ***Professional Assistance***: It
   can be helpful to engage
   professionals, such as appraisers
   or financial advisors, to assist
   with asset valuation and financial
   analysis. They can provide
   expertise to ensure accurate
   valuation and help you
   understand the financial
   implications of different division
   scenarios.

8. ***Post-Divorce Considerations***:
   After the division of assets and
   debts, it's important to update
   legal documents, such as wills,
   trusts, and beneficiary
   designations, to reflect the new
   arrangements. It's also crucial to
   close joint accounts and establish
   separate financial accounts to

manage individual finances going forward.

Remember, the division of assets and debts in a divorce can be complex, and the specific outcomes will depend on various factors. It's advisable to consult with a qualified attorney who specializes in family law to guide you through the process and ensure your rights and interests are protected.

ALIMONY AND CHILD SUPPORT

Alimony (also known as spousal support) and child support are two important financial aspects of divorce or separation that aim to address the financial needs of the individuals involved. Here's an overview of each:

1. ALIMONY/SPOUSAL SUPPORT:

- **Purpose**: Alimony is typically intended to provide financial support to a lower-earning or financially dependent spouse after divorce or separation. Its purpose is to help the recipient spouse maintain a similar standard of living to what they had during the marriage.

- **Determining Factors**: The amount and duration of alimony can vary based on several factors, including the length of the marriage, the income and earning capacity of each spouse, the standard of living during the marriage, and the recipient spouse's financial needs.

- **Types of Alimony**: Different jurisdictions may recognize different types of alimony, such as temporary alimony (during the divorce process), rehabilitative alimony (to support the recipient spouse until they become self-supporting), or permanent alimony (long-term support).

- **Modification and Termination**: Alimony orders may be subject to modification or termination under certain circumstances, such as a change in financial circumstances, cohabitation or remarriage of the recipient spouse, or the death of either party.

2. CHILD SUPPORT:

- **Purpose**: Child support is designed to ensure that both parents contribute to the financial well-being of their children after divorce or separation. It aims to cover the costs of the child's basic needs, such as food, shelter, clothing, education, healthcare, and extracurricular activities.

- **Determining Factors**: Child support calculations typically consider factors such as the income of both parents, the number of children, custody arrangements, healthcare expenses, and other relevant costs.

- **Guidelines**: Many jurisdictions have specific guidelines or formulas to calculate child support based on the aforementioned factors. These guidelines provide a framework for determining the appropriate amount of support, although deviations from the guidelines may be possible in certain cases.

- **Modification**: Child support orders may be modified if there are significant changes in either parent's financial situation or the child's needs. Common examples include changes in income, changes in custody or visitation arrangements, or medical emergencies.

It's important to note that the laws governing alimony and child support can vary by jurisdiction, and the specific rules and calculations can differ. It's advisable to consult with an attorney familiar with family law in your area to understand the specific guidelines and requirements applicable to your situation. Additionally, working with a qualified attorney or mediator can help ensure that the financial support arrangements are fair and appropriate for all parties involved.

IMPACT ON RETIREMENT SAVINGS

Divorce can have a significant impact on retirement savings for both parties involved. Here are some key considerations regarding the impact of divorce on retirement savings:

1. *Division of Retirement Assets: Retirement savings accumulated during the marriage are generally considered marital property and may be subject to division during divorce proceedings. This includes assets such as employer-sponsored retirement plans (e.g., 401(k)s, pensions), individual retirement accounts (IRAs), and other investment accounts. The*

specific rules and procedures for dividing retirement assets vary by jurisdiction.

2. ***Qualified Domestic Relations Order (QDRO)****: A QDRO is a court order that establishes the division of certain retirement assets, such as 401(k)s and pensions, between divorcing spouses. It allows for the transfer of a portion of the retirement account to the non-owning spouse without incurring early withdrawal penalties or tax consequences.*

3. ***Valuation and Distribution****: Retirement assets need to be accurately valued to determine*

their worth at the time of divorce. The division of these assets can be done in different ways, such as an equal split, a percentage-based allocation, or offsetting the value with other assets. The method of distribution depends on the specific circumstances and the laws of the jurisdiction.

4. ***Impact on Retirement Income:*** *Divorce can affect the future retirement income of both spouses. The division of retirement assets may result in a reduced retirement nest egg for each party, potentially leading to lower income in retirement. It's crucial to reassess retirement goals and financial plans in light of the changed circumstances.*

5. *Spousal Support and
   Retirement*: If spousal support
   (alimony) is awarded, it may
   have an impact on the
   retirement savings and income of
   the paying spouse. The financial
   obligation of spousal support can
   affect the ability to save for
   retirement or the amount
   available for retirement income.

6. *Social Security Benefits*:
   Divorced individuals may be
   eligible for Social Security
   benefits based on their former
   spouse's work record if they
   meet certain criteria. This can
   include spousal benefits or
   survivor benefits. Understanding
   the rules and requirements for
   Social Security benefits after

*divorce is important for
retirement planning.*

7. ***Individual Retirement
   Planning:*** *After a divorce, it is
   essential for both parties to
   reassess their individual
   retirement plans. This may
   involve consulting a financial
   advisor to adjust retirement
   savings goals, develop a new
   savings strategy, and consider
   any necessary changes to
   investment allocations.*

It's important to consult with a
qualified attorney and, if necessary, a
financial advisor who specializes in
divorce and retirement planning. They
can provide guidance tailored to your

specific situation and help you navigate
the complexities of dividing retirement
assets and planning for your financial
future.

TAX IMPLICATIONS OF DIVORCE

Divorce can have several tax implications that individuals should be aware of. Here are some common tax considerations related to divorce:

1. *Filing Status: After a divorce is finalized, individuals can no longer file their tax returns as married filing jointly or married filing separately. Instead, they will typically file as single or head of household, depending on their circumstances. Filing status can affect tax rates, deductions, and eligibility for certain tax credits.*

2. *Child-Related Tax Benefits: The custody arrangement for*

children can impact which parent is eligible to claim certain tax benefits. These benefits may include the child tax credit, the dependency exemption, the child and dependent care credit, and the earned income tax credit. The specific rules for claiming these benefits can vary, so it's important to understand the terms outlined in the divorce agreement or court orders.

3. ***Alimony and Spousal Support***: *Alimony or spousal support payments made pursuant to a divorce decree may have tax implications for both the payer and the recipient. For divorces finalized after December 31, 2018, alimony is*

no longer deductible for the payer, and the recipient does not include it as taxable income. However, for divorces finalized before that date, different rules may apply, so it's important to consult with a tax professional.

4. ***Property Transfers***: *The transfer of property between divorcing spouses may have tax consequences. Generally, transfers of property incident to divorce are tax-free, meaning they are not considered taxable events. However, it's important to evaluate the tax basis of the transferred assets, as that may affect any future capital gains taxes when the assets are sold.*

5. *Retirement Accounts*: Dividing
   retirement accounts as part of
   the divorce settlement may
   trigger tax implications. For
   example, withdrawals from
   traditional retirement accounts
   (e.g., 401(k)s, IRAs) may be
   subject to income tax, unless a
   qualified domestic relations order
   (QDRO) is used to transfer the
   funds to the other spouse's
   retirement account without
   incurring immediate tax liability.

6. *Mortgage Interest and
   Property Taxes*: If the
   divorcing couple jointly owns a
   home, they may need to consider
   the tax implications of mortgage
   interest deductions and property
   taxes. Determining who can
   claim these deductions and how

they will be allocated after the divorce should be addressed in the divorce agreement.

It's important to consult with a qualified tax professional or accountant to fully understand the tax implications of your specific divorce situation. They can provide guidance tailored to your circumstances and help ensure that you comply with applicable tax laws.

REVIEWING AND UPDATING FINANCIAL PLANS

Divorce is a significant life event that can have a substantial impact on your financial situation. It's crucial to review and update your financial plans to adapt to the changes. Here are some key steps to consider:

1. ***Assess Your Current Financial Situation***: *Start by taking stock of your current financial state. Gather information about your income, expenses, assets, debts, and any existing financial plans or investments. This will provide a clear picture of your financial standing after the divorce.*

2. ***Budgeting and Cash Flow:***
   *Create a comprehensive budget
   that reflects your new income,
   expenses, and financial
   obligations. Consider any
   changes in housing costs,
   insurance premiums, child-
   related expenses, and other
   factors that may have shifted
   due to the divorce. Make sure
   your cash flow is aligned with
   your new financial reality.*

3. ***Revisit Financial Goals:***
   *Divorce may necessitate a
   reassessment of your financial
   goals. Review your short-term
   and long-term objectives and
   adjust them based on your
   changed circumstances. This
   may include revising savings*

targets, retirement plans, education funding for children, and other financial aspirations.

4. ***Update Estate Planning Documents****: Review and update your estate planning documents, including your will, trusts, power of attorney, and healthcare directives. Ensure beneficiary designations on life insurance policies, retirement accounts, and other assets are updated to reflect your intentions after the divorce.*

5. ***Insurance Coverage****: Evaluate your insurance needs and coverage. You may need to obtain new health insurance, life*

insurance, or disability insurance policies. Adjust your coverage to meet your changing circumstances and protect yourself and your dependents adequately.

6. ***Retirement Planning:*** *Revisit your retirement plans and make any necessary adjustments. Assess the impact of the divorce on your retirement savings and projected income. Consider working with a financial advisor to help you develop a new retirement savings strategy based on your revised goals and resources.*

7. *__Investment Portfolio__: Review your investment portfolio and ensure it aligns with your updated financial goals and risk tolerance. Consider the impact of the divorce on your investment strategy and make any necessary adjustments to rebalance your portfolio.*

8. *__Seek Professional Guidance__: Divorce can be complex, and its financial implications can be overwhelming. Consider working with a financial planner or advisor who specializes in divorce and financial planning. They can provide valuable guidance, help you navigate the financial complexities, and ensure that your new financial*

plans are well-suited to your needs.

Remember, every divorce situation is unique, and it's essential to tailor your financial plans to your specific circumstances. Taking these steps can help you regain financial stability and set a solid foundation for your post-divorce financial future.

REBUILDING CREDITS AND FINANCIAL STABILITY

Divorce can have a significant impact on your credit and overall financial stability. Rebuilding your credit and achieving financial stability after a divorce may take time and effort, but it's certainly possible. Here are some steps to consider:

1. ***Assess Your Credit Situation:*** *Start by obtaining copies of your credit reports from the major credit bureaus (Equifax, Experian, and TransUnion) to understand your current credit standing. Review the reports carefully for any errors or inaccuracies.*

2. ***Address Joint Accounts and
   Debt:*** *If you had joint accounts
   or debts with your former
   spouse, it's important to address
   them appropriately. Close joint
   accounts, if possible, and work
   towards separating any joint
   debts. Consider refinancing or
   restructuring loans to remove
   your ex-spouse's name from the
   accounts.*

3. ***Establish Individual Credit:*** *If
   you don't have individual credit
   accounts in your name, start
   building your credit history.
   Apply for a credit card or a small
   personal loan in your name and
   use it responsibly. Make timely
   payments and keep your credit*

utilization low to demonstrate responsible credit management.

4. ***Pay Bills on Time****: Consistently paying your bills on time is crucial for rebuilding credit. Late or missed payments can have a negative impact on your credit score. Set up reminders or automatic payments to ensure you meet your financial obligations promptly.*

5. ***Create a Budget****: Develop a comprehensive budget to manage your expenses and income effectively. This will help you prioritize your financial obligations, track your spending,*

149

and ensure you're living within your means.

6. ***Build an Emergency Fund****: Establishing an emergency fund is essential for financial stability. Aim to save three to six months' worth of living expenses in a separate account to handle unexpected financial challenges.*

7. ***Seek Professional Guidance****: Consider working with a credit counselor or financial advisor who can provide guidance on rebuilding credit and improving your financial situation. They can help you develop a personalized plan, negotiate with creditors, and provide strategies for*

managing your finances effectively.

8. ***Monitor Your Credit****: Regularly monitor your credit reports to stay informed about your credit activity. Check for any errors, fraudulent accounts, or signs of identity theft. You can use free credit monitoring services or consider subscribing to a credit monitoring service for added protection.*

9. ***Patience and Persistence****: Rebuilding credit and achieving financial stability takes time and patience. Stay committed to responsible financial habits, consistently make payments, and*

manage your credit wisely. Over time, your credit score will improve, and your financial stability will strengthen.

Remember, rebuilding credit and achieving financial stability is a process that requires discipline and perseverance. By taking proactive steps and seeking professional guidance when needed, you can rebuild your credit and regain financial stability after a divorce.

FINANCIAL CONSIDERATION FOR ALL MAJOR LIFE EVENTS

Financial considerations are crucial for navigating major life events. Here are some key financial considerations for various significant life events:

1. MARRIAGE:

- **Combine finances or keep them separate**: Decide whether to merge your finances completely or maintain separate accounts and establish a system for managing shared expenses.

- **Update beneficiaries and insurance policies**: Review and update beneficiaries on bank accounts, retirement plans, life insurance policies, and other assets. Consider purchasing or adjusting life insurance coverage to protect your spouse.

- **Joint financial goals**: Discuss and establish common financial goals, such as saving for a house, retirement, or education expenses, and develop a plan to achieve them together.

- **Marriage tax implications**: Understand how your tax filing status may change and consult a tax professional to optimize your tax situation.

2. STARTING A FAMILY:

- **Budget for child-related expenses**: Account for costs such as childcare, education, healthcare, and other expenses when creating or adjusting your budget.

- **Review insurance coverage**: Evaluate your health insurance, life insurance, and disability insurance policies to ensure adequate coverage for your growing family.

- **Estate planning**: Create or update your wills, trusts, and guardianship designations for your children. Consider establishing a college savings plan, such as a 529 plan.

- **Emergency fund**: Build an emergency fund to cover unexpected expenses that may arise when starting a family.

3. HOMEOWNERSHIP:

- **Mortgage affordability**: Determine how much house you can afford by considering your income, existing debts, down payment, and ongoing homeownership costs like property taxes, insurance, and maintenance.

- **Credit score and mortgage rates**: Maintain a healthy credit score to secure favorable mortgage rates. Pay bills on time, manage debts responsibly, and minimize new credit applications.

- **Home insurance**: Obtain adequate homeowners insurance coverage to protect your property and belongings.

- **Home maintenance and repairs**: Budget for ongoing home maintenance and repairs, as they are inevitable expenses of homeownership.

4. CAREER CHANGES:

- **Salary and benefits**: Evaluate the financial impact of a potential career change, including changes in salary, benefits, and retirement plans.

- **Training and education costs**: Consider the cost of acquiring new skills, certifications, or additional education required for the career change.

- **Health insurance**: Assess the availability and cost of health insurance coverage during and after the transition.

- **Unemployment protection**: Save for a financial cushion to cover expenses during potential periods of unemployment or lower income when transitioning careers.

5. RETIREMENT:

- **Retirement savings**: Save consistently for retirement by contributing to retirement accounts like 401(k)s, IRAs, or pension plans.

- **Investment strategy**: Develop an investment strategy aligned with your retirement goals, risk tolerance, and time horizon. Review and adjust your investment portfolio regularly.

- **Health care costs**: Plan for potential healthcare costs in retirement, including long-term care insurance or health savings accounts (HSAs).

- **Social Security and pension benefits**: Understand the implications of claiming Social Security benefits and any pension benefits you may be eligible for.

These considerations are not exhaustive, and each life event will have unique financial implications. It's essential to consult with financial professionals, such as financial advisors, tax professionals, or estate planners, to ensure you make informed decisions and optimize your financial situation during major life events.

EMERGENCY FUND AND FINANCIAL SAFETY NET

Having an emergency fund and a financial safety net is crucial for all major life events. Here's why they are important and how you can establish and maintain them:

1. EMERGENCY FUND:

- **Purpose**: An emergency fund is a savings account specifically set aside to cover unexpected expenses or financial emergencies. It provides a financial cushion and helps you avoid going into debt when unexpected costs arise.

- **Recommended Amount**: Aim to save three to six months' worth of living expenses in your emergency fund. This should cover essential expenses like housing, food, utilities, transportation, and debt payments in case of job loss or other emergencies.

- **Building Your Emergency Fund**:

- **Start small and be consistent**: Set a realistic savings goal and contribute regularly to your emergency fund. Even small amounts add up over time.
- **Automate savings**: Set up automatic transfers from your paycheck or checking account to your emergency fund to ensure consistent savings.
- **Cut expenses**: Look for areas in your budget where you can reduce spending

and allocate those savings to your emergency fund.

○ **Windfalls and bonuses**: *Direct unexpected or extra income, such as tax refunds or work bonuses, towards your emergency fund.*

- Accessing Your Emergency Fund: Keep your emergency fund in a separate, easily accessible account, such as a high-yield savings account. This ensures you can quickly access the funds when needed.

2. FINANCIAL SAFETY NET:

- Insurance Coverage: Protect yourself and your family with appropriate insurance coverage, including health insurance, life insurance, disability insurance, and

property and casualty insurance.
Evaluate your coverage regularly to
ensure it aligns with your needs.

- **Adequate Retirement Savings**:
Building a robust retirement savings is
a critical part of your financial safety
net. Contribute consistently to
retirement accounts such as 401(k)s,
IRAs, or pension plans to secure your
future.

- **Debt Management**: Minimize and
manage your debt, such as credit card
debt, student loans, or mortgages.
Establish a plan to pay off high-interest
debt and avoid taking on excessive
debt.

- **Diversify Income Streams**:
Having multiple sources of income can
provide additional financial security.
Explore opportunities for side gigs,
freelance work, or investments to

diversify your income and reduce
reliance on a single source.

Remember, emergencies can come in
various forms, such as job loss,
medical expenses, car repairs, or home
repairs. By having an emergency fund
and a solid financial safety net, you
can navigate these unforeseen events
without derailing your financial stability
or resorting to high-interest debt.
Regularly reassess and adjust your
emergency fund and financial safety
net as your circumstances change to
ensure they remain adequate for your
needs.

REVIEWING AND UPDATING INSURANCE COVERAGE

Reviewing and updating insurance coverage is an essential financial consideration for all major life events. Here's a guide on how to approach insurance coverage during significant life changes:

1. MARRIAGE:

- **Health Insurance**: Evaluate the health insurance plans available to both spouses and determine which one offers the most comprehensive coverage at the best cost. Consider joining a spousal health insurance plan if available.

- **Life Insurance**: Review your life insurance needs and consider purchasing or updating policies to ensure adequate coverage for both spouses. Assess beneficiaries and make any necessary changes.

- **Homeowner's/Renter's Insurance**: If you or your spouse will be moving or combining households, review and update your homeowner's or renter's insurance policies to reflect the new living arrangement.

2. STARTING A FAMILY:

- **Health Insurance**: Review your health insurance coverage to understand maternity/paternity benefits, pediatric care, and any associated costs. Ensure that your insurance adequately covers prenatal care, delivery, and pediatric visits.

- **Life Insurance**: Assess your life insurance needs and consider increasing coverage to provide financial protection for your growing family.

- **Disability Insurance**: Evaluate disability insurance coverage to protect your income in case of a disability that prevents you from working.

- **Homeowner's Insurance**: Update your homeowner's insurance policy to reflect any changes in your home, such as added square footage or increased value due to renovations.

3. HOMEOWNERSHIP:

- **Homeowner's Insurance**: Obtain or update your homeowner's insurance policy to adequately cover your new property's value and any improvements or additions.

- **Flood Insurance**: Assess the need for flood insurance, depending on the property's location and flood risk. Consider purchasing flood insurance separately if it is not covered by your homeowner's insurance policy.

- **Title Insurance**: When purchasing a new home, consider obtaining title insurance to protect against any legal issues or disputes regarding the property's ownership.

4. CAREER CHANGES:

- **Health Insurance**: Evaluate your health insurance options when transitioning careers. Understand the coverage provided by potential employers or explore individual health insurance plans if necessary.

- **Disability Insurance**: Assess disability insurance coverage to ensure you have income protection in case of a career change that results in a loss of benefits provided by your previous employer.

- **Professional Liability Insurance**: If starting a new business or going into a self-employed role, consider professional liability insurance to protect against potential claims or lawsuits related to your professional services.

5. RETIREMENT:

- **Health Insurance**: Understand your health insurance options after retirement, including Medicare coverage, supplemental plans, and long-term care insurance.

- **Life Insurance:** Evaluate your life insurance needs in retirement. Determine if you need to maintain coverage to provide for your spouse or dependents or adjust coverage based on changes in financial responsibilities.

- **Long-Term Care Insurance**: Consider long-term care insurance to protect against the high costs of extended care services that may be needed in later years.

Remember to regularly review and update your insurance coverage as your life circumstances change. Consult with insurance professionals to ensure you have the appropriate coverage to protect yourself, your family, and your assets during significant life events.

ESTATE PLANNING AND WILL PREPARATION

Estate planning and will preparation are crucial financial considerations for all major life events. Here's a guide on how to approach estate planning and will preparation during significant life changes:

1. MARRIAGE:

- **Update Beneficiaries**: Review and update beneficiaries on your bank accounts, retirement plans, life insurance policies, and other assets to reflect your spouse's new role in your life.

- **Joint Wills or Individual Wills**: Consider whether you and your spouse will create a joint will or maintain separate individual wills. Consult with an estate planning attorney to understand the implications and which option is most suitable for your situation.

   - **Power of Attorney and Healthcare Proxy**: Designate your spouse as your power of attorney and healthcare proxy to make financial and medical decisions on your behalf if you become incapacitated.

2. STARTING A FAMILY:

   - **Guardianship Designation**: Determine who will take care of your children if something happens to both parents. Designate guardians in your will to ensure their well-being and care.

   - **Trusts**: Consider setting up trusts to manage and protect assets for your children's future, ensuring they are used for their intended purposes, such as education or healthcare.

- **Life Insurance**: Assess your life insurance coverage to provide financial support for your children's needs and future expenses.

3. HOMEOWNERSHIP:

- **Property Distribution**: Determine how you would like your property and assets to be distributed upon your death. Specify in your will who will inherit your home or other properties.

- **Considerations for Joint Ownership**: If you own a property jointly with someone other than your spouse, consider how your share of the property will be distributed and address it in your estate plan.

4. CAREER CHANGES:

- **Update Beneficiaries and Estate Plans**: Review and update your beneficiaries and estate plans to reflect any changes in assets, retirement plans, or life insurance policies resulting from your career change.

- **Address Stock Options or Equity**: If you have stock options or equity in a company, determine how these assets will be handled in your estate plan.

5. RETIREMENT:

- **Retirement Accounts**: Ensure that your retirement accounts, such as 401(k)s or IRAs, have designated beneficiaries and are aligned with your estate plan.

- **Healthcare Directives**: Establish healthcare directives, such as a living will or medical power of attorney, to outline your preferences for medical treatment and designate someone to make healthcare decisions on your behalf if you are unable to do so.

It is highly recommended to consult with an experienced estate planning attorney to ensure your estate plan and will accurately reflect your wishes and comply with legal requirements. They can provide personalized guidance based on your unique circumstances and help you navigate the complexities of estate planning and will preparation. Regularly review and update your estate plan as your life circumstances change to ensure it remains current and aligned with your intentions.

BUILDING AND MAINTAINING A GOOD CREDIT SCORE

Building and maintaining a good credit score is an important financial consideration for all major life events. A good credit score can positively impact your ability to secure loans, obtain favorable interest rates, rent an apartment, or even land a job. Here's a guide on how to build and maintain a good credit score:

1. ESTABLISH CREDIT:

- **Open a Credit Account**: Start by opening a credit account, such as a credit card or a small personal loan. Consider secured credit cards if you have limited or no credit history.

- **Become an Authorized User**: If possible, become an authorized user on someone else's credit card with a good payment history. This can help establish credit history.

2. MAKE TIMELY PAYMENTS:

- **Pay on Time**: Always make your credit card, loan, and other debt payments on time. Late or missed payments can significantly impact your credit score.

- **Set Up Payment Reminders**: Utilize payment reminders, automatic payments, or calendar alerts to ensure you never miss a payment.

3. KEEP CREDIT UTILIZATION LOW:

- **Use Credit Wisely**: Keep your credit card balances low and avoid maxing out your credit limits. Aim to use less than 30% of your available credit.

- **Pay in Full**: Whenever possible, pay your credit card balances in full each month to avoid accruing high-interest charges.

4. MAINTAIN A DIVERSE CREDIT MIX:

- **Have Different Types of Credit**: Maintain a mix of credit accounts, such as credit cards, installment loans, and a mortgage if applicable. This demonstrates your ability to handle various types of credit responsibly.

5. MONITOR YOUR CREDIT REPORT:

   - **Obtain Free Credit Reports**: Regularly review your credit reports from the major credit bureaus (Equifax, Experian, and TransUnion). You are entitled to a free annual credit report from each bureau.

   - **Check for Errors**: Review your credit reports for inaccuracies, such as incorrect accounts or late payments. Dispute any errors you find to have them corrected promptly.

6. LIMIT NEW CREDIT APPLICATIONS:

   - **Be Selective**: Avoid applying for multiple credit accounts within a short period. Each application generates a hard inquiry, which can temporarily lower your credit score.

7. MAINTAIN A LONG CREDIT HISTORY:

- **Keep Old Accounts Open**: Length of credit history is an essential factor in determining your credit score. Keep older credit accounts open and active, even if you don't frequently use them.

8. BE RESPONSIBLE WITH CO-SIGNED ACCOUNTS:

- **Understand Co-Signing Implications**: If you co-sign a loan or credit account, understand that it will impact your credit score as well. Ensure the primary borrower makes timely payments to avoid negative consequences.

Remember, building and maintaining a good credit score takes time and discipline. It's important to be patient and consistent in your credit management habits. By establishing good credit habits early on and consistently practicing responsible credit behavior, you can build and maintain a strong credit score that will serve you well in various financial situations.

BUDGETING AND FINANCIAL DISCIPLINE

Budgeting and maintaining financial discipline are essential considerations for all major life events. Effective budgeting helps you manage your finances, achieve your goals, and make informed financial decisions. Here's a guide on how to approach budgeting and maintain financial discipline during significant life changes:

1. ASSESS YOUR FINANCIAL SITUATION:

- **Track Income and Expenses**: Start by understanding your current financial situation. Track your income and expenses to determine where your money is going.

- **Evaluate Debts and Liabilities**: Take stock of your debts, including loans, credit card balances, and other liabilities. Understand the interest rates and terms associated with each debt.

2. SET FINANCIAL GOALS:

- **Short-Term and Long-Term Goals**: Identify your financial goals and prioritize them. This could include saving for emergencies, paying off debt, saving for a down payment on a home, or planning for retirement.

- **SMART Goals**: Make your goals Specific, Measurable, Achievable, Relevant, and Time-bound. This helps you create a clear plan and track your progress.

3. CREATE A BUDGET:

- **Income and Expenses**: Determine your monthly income from all sources. Then, categorize your expenses into essential categories (such as housing, utilities, and groceries) and discretionary categories (such as entertainment and dining out).

- **Allocate Funds**: Allocate your income to each expense category based on your priorities. Ensure that you have enough to cover essential expenses while also contributing to savings and debt repayment.

- **Track and Adjust**: Regularly track your expenses and compare them to your budget to identify areas where you can cut back or make adjustments.

4. REDUCE EXPENSES:

- **Cut Back on Discretionary Spending**: Identify areas where you can reduce discretionary spending, such as eating out less frequently, canceling unnecessary subscriptions, or finding cost-effective alternatives for entertainment.

- **Negotiate Bills and Expenses**: Review your bills and negotiate lower rates where possible. This could include negotiating better rates for utilities, insurance policies, or cable/internet services.

5. BUILD AN EMERGENCY FUND:

- **Save for Emergencies**: Establish an emergency fund to cover unexpected expenses, such as medical bills or car repairs. Aim to save three to six months' worth of living expenses.

   - **Automate Savings**: Set up automatic transfers from your checking account to a separate savings account to ensure consistent savings contributions.

6. MANAGE DEBT:

   - **Prioritize Debt Repayment**: Allocate extra funds towards paying off high-interest debt to reduce interest payments and become debt-free faster. Consider using strategies such as the debt avalanche or debt snowball method.

   - **Avoid New Debt**: Be cautious about taking on new debt unless necessary. Consider the long-term impact on your budget before financing a major purchase.

7. REVIEW AND ADJUST REGULARLY:

   - **Regularly Review Your Budget**: Review your budget periodically to ensure it aligns with your changing financial circumstances and goals. Make adjustments as needed.

   - **Celebrate Milestones**: Celebrate your financial achievements along the way. This helps maintain motivation and reinforces positive financial habits.

Maintaining financial discipline requires consistency and self-control. Stay committed to your budget, be mindful of your spending habits, and make intentional choices that align with your financial goals. Regularly reassess your budget and make adjustments as needed. By practicing financial

discipline, you can achieve financial
stability and make informed decisions
during all major life events.

SEEKING PROFESSIONAL FINANCIAL ADVICE

Seeking professional financial advice is a crucial consideration for all major life events. Financial advisors can provide valuable guidance, expertise, and personalized strategies to help you navigate complex financial decisions and achieve your financial goals. Here's a guide on when and how to seek professional financial advice:

1. WHEN TO SEEK PROFESSIONAL FINANCIAL ADVICE:

- **Significant Life Events**: Consider seeking professional advice during major life events such as marriage, starting a family, buying a home, changing careers, planning for retirement, or receiving a significant inheritance.

- **Complex Financial Situations**: If you have complex financial situations like managing multiple income sources, dealing with substantial investments, or planning for business ownership, seeking professional advice can be beneficial.

- **Long-Term Financial Planning**: Financial advisors can assist with long-term financial planning, including retirement planning, investment strategies, and estate planning.

2. CHOOSING A FINANCIAL ADVISOR:

- **Credentials and Qualifications:** Look for financial advisors who are certified, such as Certified Financial

Planner (CFP) professionals. They typically have the knowledge and expertise to provide comprehensive financial advice.

- **Fee Structure**: Understand the fee structure of the financial advisor. They may charge a flat fee, hourly rate, or a percentage of assets under management (AUM). Choose a fee structure that aligns with your needs and budget.

- **Fiduciary Duty**: Consider working with a fiduciary financial advisor who is legally obligated to act in your best interest.

3. FINANCIAL PLANNING PROCESS:

- **Initial Consultation**: Schedule an initial consultation with a financial advisor to discuss your financial goals, concerns, and expectations. This meeting helps you evaluate if the advisor is a good fit for your needs.

- **Comprehensive Assessment**: A financial advisor will conduct a thorough assessment of your financial situation, including income, expenses, assets, liabilities, and investment portfolio.

- **Goal Setting and Strategies**: Based on your assessment, the advisor will help you set realistic financial goals and develop personalized strategies to achieve them. This may include investment planning, tax strategies, retirement planning, or estate planning.

- **Regular Reviews and Updates**: A good financial advisor will provide ongoing support and conduct regular reviews of your financial plan to ensure it remains aligned with your changing circumstances and goals.

193

4. COLLABORATE WITH OTHER PROFESSIONALS:

- **Team Approach**: In complex financial situations, it may be beneficial to work with a team of professionals, including financial advisors, tax professionals, estate planning attorneys, and insurance experts, to address various aspects of your financial planning.

- **Coordination and Collaboration**: Ensure that your financial advisor collaborates and coordinates with other professionals to create a comprehensive and cohesive financial plan.

Remember, financial advisors are there to provide guidance and expertise, but ultimately, you are responsible for making decisions about your finances. Be prepared to share relevant information about your financial situation and personal goals to help your advisor develop suitable strategies. Regularly communicate with your financial advisor and be proactive in seeking their advice during important financial decisions or life events.

CONCLUSION

In conclusion, considering financial aspects is crucial during all major life events. Building and maintaining a good credit score, practicing budgeting and financial discipline, and seeking professional financial advice are key considerations that can help you make informed decisions and achieve your financial goals.

Building a good credit score involves establishing credit, making timely payments, keeping credit utilization low, maintaining a diverse credit mix, monitoring your credit report, limiting new credit applications, and maintaining a long credit history. A good credit score opens doors to favorable loan terms, lower interest

rates, and various financial
opportunities.

Budgeting and financial discipline play
a vital role in managing your finances
effectively. By assessing your financial
situation, setting goals, creating a
budget, reducing expenses, building an
emergency fund, managing debt, and
reviewing and adjusting regularly, you
can establish healthy financial habits
and work towards your financial
objectives.

Seeking professional financial advice is
essential during major life events,
complex financial situations, and long-
term financial planning. Choosing a
qualified financial advisor, collaborating
with other professionals as needed,
and going through the financial

planning process can provide valuable insights, personalized strategies, and peace of mind.

Remember, everyone's financial situation is unique, and it's important to tailor financial considerations to your specific circumstances. By being proactive, informed, and disciplined in managing your finances, you can navigate major life events with confidence and set yourself up for long-term financial success.

RECAP OF KEY POINTS

Certainly! Here's a recap of the key points regarding the financial impact of major life events such as marriage, parenthood, and divorce:

1. MARRIAGE:

  - **Joint Financial Planning**: Create a joint budget and financial plan with your spouse to align your financial goals and priorities.

  - **Combine Finances**: Decide whether to merge your bank accounts, credit cards, and other financial accounts. Consider the best approach for your situation.

  - **Update Legal Documents**: Review and update beneficiary

designations, wills, and other legal documents to reflect your marital status and wishes.

- **Consider Insurance Needs**: Assess your insurance coverage, including health, life, and disability insurance, and make any necessary adjustments.

2. PARENTHOOD:

- **Budget for New Expenses**: Anticipate and plan for the additional costs associated with raising a child, including childcare, education, healthcare, and everyday essentials.

- **Review Insurance Coverage**: Evaluate your health insurance coverage and consider adding or adjusting life insurance policies to provide financial protection for your child.

- **Start Saving for College**: Explore options for saving for your child's education, such as a 529 college savings plan or other investment vehicles.

- **Update Legal and Financial Documents**: Update your wills, guardianship designations, and beneficiary designations to reflect your child's arrival.

3. DIVORCE:

- **Understand the Financial Implications**: Familiarize yourself with the financial aspects of divorce, including property division, alimony, child support, and potential changes in income and expenses.

- **Seek Professional Guidance**: Consult with a divorce attorney and, if necessary, a financial advisor who specializes in divorce to help you navigate the process and protect your financial interests.

- **Separate Finances**: Establish separate bank accounts and credit cards to disentangle your finances from your ex-spouse.

- **Update Legal and Financial Documents**: Revise your will, beneficiary designations, and other legal documents to reflect the changes in your marital status and wishes.

It's important to note that these are general considerations, and the specific financial impact of these life events can vary depending on individual circumstances. Seeking professional advice from financial experts and legal professionals is recommended to ensure you make well-informed

decisions that align with your unique
situation and goals.

IMPORTANCE OF PROACTIVE FINANCIAL PLANNING

Proactive financial planning is crucial for several reasons. Here are the key reasons highlighting the importance of proactive financial planning:

1. *Goal Setting and Achievement: Proactive financial planning allows you to set clear financial goals and develop a roadmap to achieve them. It helps you identify what you want to accomplish financially and provides actionable steps to reach those goals.*

2. *Financial Security and Stability*: By proactively planning your finances, you can build a strong financial foundation and increase your overall financial security. This includes creating emergency funds, managing debt, and establishing appropriate insurance coverage to protect yourself and your loved ones from unexpected events.

3. *Maximizing Opportunities*: Being proactive allows you to identify and take advantage of financial opportunities. Whether it's investing in the stock market, real estate, or starting a business, proactive financial planning helps you make

informed decisions to grow your wealth and make the most of favorable circumstances.

4. ***Effective Resource Allocation:*** *Proactive financial planning helps you allocate your financial resources wisely. By tracking income and expenses, creating budgets, and making informed spending decisions, you can optimize your financial resources and avoid unnecessary expenditures or wasteful habits.*

5. ***Adaptation to Changing Circumstances:*** *Life is full of unexpected changes and events. Proactive financial planning equips you with the ability to*

adapt to these changes effectively. Whether it's a career transition, a medical emergency, or a major life event, having a financial plan in place can provide a sense of stability and guide you through uncertain times.

6. **Retirement Planning**: *Planning for retirement is a critical aspect of financial planning. Being proactive allows you to start saving and investing early, take advantage of retirement accounts and employer-sponsored plans, and make informed decisions about when and how to retire comfortably.*

7. *Peace of Mind*: *Proactive
   financial planning reduces
   financial stress and provides
   peace of mind. Knowing that you
   have a plan in place,
   contingencies accounted for, and
   a roadmap to achieve your
   financial goals can alleviate
   anxiety and help you focus on
   other important aspects of your
   life.*

Remember, proactive financial
planning is an ongoing process.
Regularly reviewing and adjusting your
financial plan as circumstances change
is essential to ensure it remains
relevant and effective. Seeking the
guidance of a financial advisor or
planner can further enhance your
proactive approach, as they can
provide expertise, insights, and

objective advice tailored to your
specific financial situation and goals.

TAKING CONTROL OF YOUR FINANCIAL FUTURE

Taking control of your financial future is empowering and can greatly impact your overall well-being. Here are key steps to help you take control of your financial future:

1. *Assess Your Current Financial Situation: Start by evaluating your current financial status. Take stock of your income, expenses, debts, assets, and savings. Understand where your money is going and identify areas for improvement.*

2. *Set Clear Financial Goals: Define your short-term and long-*

term financial goals. Be specific about what you want to achieve, such as saving for a down payment on a house, paying off debt, or building a retirement fund. Having clear goals will give you direction and motivation.

3. **Create a Budget**: Develop a realistic budget that aligns with your financial goals. Track your income and expenses, and allocate your money accordingly. Prioritize essential expenses, reduce discretionary spending, and find areas to save more.

4. **Build an Emergency Fund**: Establish an emergency fund to cover unexpected expenses. Aim

*to save three to six months'
worth of living expenses. Having
this safety net provides financial
security and reduces the need to
rely on credit or loans during
emergencies.*

5. ***Manage and Reduce Debt:***
   *Take control of your debt by
   understanding your outstanding
   balances, interest rates, and
   repayment terms. Develop a
   strategy to pay off your debts
   systematically, starting with
   high-interest debts first.
   Consider debt consolidation or
   refinancing options if it can help
   you save money.*

6. **Save and Invest**: *Make saving a priority. Set aside a portion of your income for savings and investments. Start with small amounts and gradually increase your contributions. Explore investment options such as retirement accounts, stocks, bonds, or real estate to grow your wealth over time.*

7. **Educate Yourself**: *Take the time to educate yourself about personal finance. Read books, attend workshops, or follow reputable financial blogs to gain knowledge and make informed financial decisions. Understanding concepts like budgeting, investing, and retirement planning will empower*

*you to take control of your
financial future.*

8. ***Review and Adjust Regularly****:
   Financial circumstances change
   over time, so it's important to
   review and adjust your financial
   plan regularly. Revisit your goals,
   budget, and investments
   periodically to ensure they align
   with your evolving needs and life
   events.*

9. ***Seek Professional Advice****:
   Consider working with a financial
   advisor or planner. They can
   provide expert guidance, help
   you develop a personalized
   financial plan, and offer valuable*

10.   ***Stay Disciplined and Persistent***: *Taking control of your financial future requires discipline and persistence. Stay committed to your goals, stay on track with your budget, and make consistent efforts to improve your financial situation.*

Remember, taking control of your financial future is a journey. It may take time and effort, but the rewards of financial security, stability, and freedom are worth it. Start today, stay focused, and celebrate your progress along the way.

215